South Beach Diet CookBook

Deliciously Quick & Easy Recipes You Can Make Within Minutes

Mia Sullivan

Table Of Contents:

<u>INTRODUCTION</u>

The South Beach Diet Experience

Have you ever heard of the South Beach Diet? It's this awesome way of eating that's been around since the early 2000s and is all about being healthy. Imagine this: balanced meals with good stuff like whole foods, lean proteins, healthy fats, and low-glycemic carbs. It's not just about dropping pounds; it's about making a lifelong commitment to feeling great through what you eat.

Cooking Made Quick and Easy: Your Kitchen Sidekick

Life these days can be crazy busy, right? Finding time to cook healthy meals might feel like a puzzle. But hey, don't worry, this cookbook is here to help. I've gathered a bunch of delicious, wholesome recipes that you can whip up in just 30 minutes or less. I totally get that your time is precious, and my mission is to show you that cooking nutritious food can be both easy and super tasty.

No More Kitchen Jitters

If you're not exactly a pro in the kitchen, no sweat. I've got your back. I've included some kitchen basics and cooking tips to help you feel confident and comfortable. From handling knives to swapping ingredients, I've got you covered. So, whether you're a seasoned cook or just getting started, you'll find some cool tips to boost your kitchen skills.

From Morning to Night: Let's Eat!

This cookbook is packed with recipes that cover your entire day. Kickstart your mornings with Breakfast Boosts that'll give you energy to face that morning hustle and bustle. When those midday cravings hit, dive into Snacks in a Snap. Lunchtime? I've put out a list of Light and Fresh Salads that'll satisfy you. For dinner, explore Quick and Flavorful Seafood, Speedy Poultry Dishes, and Fast and Satisfying Meats. And don't miss out on Quick Veggie Delights and Speedy Sides to complete your meals. Oh, and guess what? There are Effortless Desserts to treat your sweet tooth and Refreshing Beverages to keep you cool.

This is not just a cookbook; it's your ticket to the fantastic world of healthy eating that also tastes amazing. Get ready to enjoy every bite, take care of your body, and have a blast cooking up meals that are quick and seriously satisfying. Ready, set, let's get cooking!

Chapter 1: BREAKFAST BOOSTS

You can jumpstart your day with these quick and delicious breakfast options that will keep you satisfied and ready to take on whatever comes your way.

Speedy Scrambled Eggs with Spinach and Feta

Prep Time: 10 minutes | Cook Time: 5 minutes | Servings: 2

Ingredients

- 2 large eggs

- 1 cup fresh spinach, chopped

- 1/4 cup crumbled feta cheese

- Salt and pepper to taste

- Cooking spray

Instruction

1. In a bowl, whisk the eggs until well combined. Season with a pinch of salt and a dash of pepper.

2. Heat a non-stick skillet over medium heat and lightly coat with cooking spray.

3. Add the chopped spinach to the skillet and sauté for about 1-2 minutes until wilted.

4. Pour the whisked eggs into the skillet over the spinach.

5. Gently scramble the eggs with a spatula as they cook, pushing them from the edges towards the center.

6. When the eggs are almost set, sprinkle the crumbled feta cheese.

7. Continue cooking for another 1-2 minutes until the eggs are fully cooked and the cheese is melted.

8. Slide the scrambled eggs onto a plate and serve hot.

Health Benefits

-*Protein Boost:* Eggs are an excellent source of high-quality protein, which helps in muscle repair and growth.

-*Leafy Greens Goodness:* Spinach provides a rich source of vitamins and minerals, including iron, vitamin K, and folate, which support overall health.

-*Bone Health:* Feta cheese contributes calcium and phosphorus, essential for maintaining strong bones.

Greek Yogurt Parfait with Fresh Berries

Prep Time: 8 minutes | No Cooking Required | Servings: 2

Ingredients:

- 1 cup plain Greek yogurt

- 1/2 cup mixed berries (strawberries, blueberries, raspberries)

- 2 tablespoons honey

- 2 tablespoons granola

Instructions

1. In a glass or bowl, layer half of the Greek yogurt.

2. Add a layer of mixed berries on top of the yogurt.

3. Drizzle 1 tablespoon of honey over the berries.

4. Layer the remaining Greek yogurt over the berries.

5. Top with the remaining mixed berries.

6. Drizzle the remaining honey over the top and sprinkle with granola.

7. Grab a spoon and enjoy this delightful and nutritious parfait!

Health Benefits

Probiotic Power: Greek yogurt is a probiotic-rich food that supports a healthy gut by promoting beneficial gut bacteria.

Antioxidant-Rich. Berries are packed with antioxidants that help combat inflammation and oxidative stress in the body.

Fiber Boost: The combination of yogurt and berries provides dietary fiber, aiding digestion and promoting a feeling of fullness.

Nutty Breakfast Quinoa Bowl

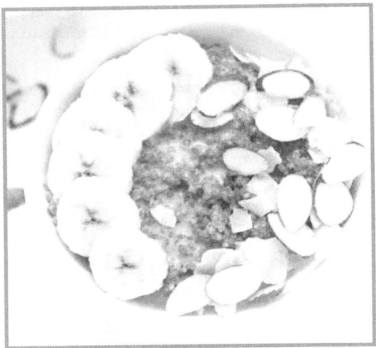

Prep Time: 5 minutes | Cook Time: 15 minutes | Servings: 2

Ingredients

- 1/2 cup cooked quinoa

- 1/4 cup chopped nuts (almonds, walnuts, or your choice)

- 1/2 banana, sliced

- 1 tablespoon chia seeds

- 1/2 cup unsweetened almond milk

- 1 teaspoon honey

Instructions

1. In a bowl, combine the cooked quinoa and chopped nuts.

2. Arrange the banana slices on top of the quinoa-nut mixture.

3. Sprinkle chia seeds over the bananas.

4. Pour unsweetened almond milk over the ingredients in the bowl.

5. Drizzle honey on top for a touch of sweetness.

6. Give it a gentle stir before digging in to enjoy a satisfying and protein-packed breakfast.

Health Benefits

Complete Protein: Quinoa is a plant-based complete protein, containing all essential amino acids needed by the body.

Heart-Healthy Fats: Nuts contribute healthy fats, including monounsaturated and polyunsaturated fats, which support heart health.

Omega-3 Fatty Acids: Chia seeds are a source of omega-3 fatty acids, beneficial for brain health and reducing inflammation.

Veggie-Packed Breakfast Burritos

Prep Time: 15 minutes | Cook Time: 10 minutes | Servings: 4

Ingredients

- 2 whole wheat tortillas

- 4 large eggs, beaten

- 1/2 cup bell peppers, diced

- 1/4 cup red onion, diced

- 1/2 cup black beans, drained and rinsed

- 1/4 cup reduced-fat shredded cheddar cheese

- Salt and pepper to taste

- Salsa (optional, for serving)

Instructions

1. In a non-stick skillet, sauté diced bell peppers and red onion until they are tender, about 3-4 minutes.

2. Add beaten eggs to the skillet and scramble them with the vegetables until cooked.

3. Warm the whole wheat tortillas in a dry skillet or microwave for a few seconds.

4. Divide the scrambled egg mixture between the tortillas.

5. Top each tortilla with black beans and shredded cheddar cheese.

6. Season with salt and pepper to taste.

7. Roll up the tortillas into burritos, folding in the sides as you go.

8. Serve with salsa on the side for an extra kick of flavor.

Health Benefits

Fiber-Rich. Whole wheat tortillas and black beans provide dietary fiber that aids digestion, regulates blood sugar, and supports weight management.

Vitamins and Minerals. Bell peppers and onions are rich in vitamins A and C, which boost the immune system and promote healthy skin.

Versatile Protein. Black beans offer plant-based protein that is low in fat and high in fiber, contributing to satiety.

By incorporating these Breakfast Boosts into your morning routine, you're not only starting your day with delicious flavors but also providing your body with essential nutrients, proteins, and healthy fats. These recipes are designed to keep you energized, satisfied, and on track for a successful day ahead.

Overall Benefits of Your First Meal Of The Day

1. *Enhanced Energy Levels:* Breakfast is often referred to as the "most important meal of the day" because it provides the body with the essential nutrients and fuel it needs after an overnight fast. A well-balanced breakfast, like the Breakfast Boosts recipes, can replenish glycogen stores and provide a steady source of energy to kick-start your day.

2. *Improved Focus and Concentration:* Nutrient-rich breakfasts can support cognitive function, helping you stay alert and focused throughout the morning. Foods high in complex carbohydrates, proteins, and healthy fats, such as those found in Breakfast Boosts, provide a sustained release of energy to the brain.

3. *Support for Weight Management:* Eating a nutritious breakfast can help regulate appetite and prevent overeating later in the day. The protein and fiber content in many Breakfast Boosts recipes contribute to feelings of fullness, reducing the likelihood of unhealthy snacking and excessive calorie intake.

4. *Better Nutrient Intake:* Breakfast is an opportunity to consume essential nutrients that may be lacking in other meals. The diverse ingredients in Breakfast Boosts recipes, such as fruits, vegetables, whole grains, lean proteins, and healthy fats, contribute to a well-rounded nutrient intake.

5. *Metabolism Boost:* Consuming breakfast can kickstart your metabolism, as it signals to your body that it's time to start burning calories for energy. The metabolism-boosting effects can be further enhanced by including protein-rich foods, as they have a higher thermic effect, meaning your body burns more calories to digest them.

6. *Balanced Blood Sugar Levels:* A balanced breakfast can help stabilize blood sugar levels, preventing the sharp spikes and crashes that can occur when meals are skipped. The fiber and complex carbohydrates in Breakfast Boosts recipes are digested more slowly, leading to a gradual rise in blood sugar.

7. *Heart Health:* Certain components of Breakfast Boosts, such as whole grains, nuts, seeds, and healthy fats, contribute to heart health. These ingredients can help lower LDL (bad) cholesterol levels, reduce inflammation, and support overall cardiovascular function.

8. *Muscle Maintenance and Repair:* Protein is essential for muscle maintenance, repair, and growth. Including protein-rich sources in Breakfast Boosts, such as eggs, Greek yogurt, and nuts, provides the amino acids needed for these processes.

9. *Digestive Health:* Many Breakfast Boosts recipes contain dietary fiber, which supports healthy digestion and helps prevent constipation. Fiber also promotes a diverse and beneficial gut microbiome, which is linked to various aspects of health.

10. *Positive Mood:* Nutrient-dense breakfasts can contribute to a positive mood by providing essential vitamins and minerals that play a role in brain health. Additionally, stabilizing blood

sugar levels through a balanced breakfast can help prevent mood swings and irritability.

Chapter 2: SNACKS IN A SNAP

When hunger strikes between meals, don't reach for those unhealthy, store-bought snacks. Instead, dive into these Snacks in a Snap – quick, easy, and satisfying bites that keep you energized and on track with your diet

Zesty Guacamole and Veggie Sticks

Prep Time: 15 minutes | No Cooking Required | Servings: 4

Ingredients

- 2 ripe avocados, peeled, pitted, and mashed

- 1 small tomato, diced

- 1/4 cup red onion, finely chopped

- 1 garlic clove, minced

- Juice of 1 lime

- 1/4 teaspoon cayenne pepper (adjust to taste)

- Salt and pepper to taste

- Assorted vegetable sticks (carrots, celery, bell peppers) for dipping

---

Instructions

1. In a bowl, combine the mashed avocados, diced tomato, chopped red onion, minced garlic, lime juice, and cayenne pepper.

2. Mix until well incorporated. Season with salt and pepper.

3. Serve the guacamole with an array of colorful vegetable sticks for a refreshing and nutritious snack.

Health Benefits

Heart-Healthy Fats: Avocado, the main ingredient in guacamole, contains monounsaturated fats that can help lower bad cholesterol levels and support heart health.

Vitamins and Minerals: Avocado is rich in potassium, which supports healthy blood pressure levels, and vitamins E and C, which act as antioxidants.

Fiber Boost: The combination of guacamole and veggie sticks provides dietary fiber that aids digestion and supports weight management.

Spiced Nuts for On-the-Go

Prep Time: 5 minutes | Cook Time: 10 minutes | Servings: 8

Ingredients

- 1 cup mixed nuts (almonds, walnuts, pecans)

- 1 tablespoon olive oil

- 1/2 teaspoon ground cumin

- 1/2 teaspoon paprika

- 1/4 teaspoon cayenne pepper

- Salt to taste

Instructions

1. Preheat the oven to 350°F (175°C).

2. In a bowl, toss the mixed nuts with olive oil, ground cumin, paprika, cayenne pepper, and salt.

3. Spread the seasoned nuts on a baking sheet in a single layer.

4. Bake for about 10-12 minutes, stirring once, until the nuts are toasted and fragrant.

5. Let them cool before enjoying this spiced and crunchy snack.

Health Benefits

Healthy Fats: Nuts are a great source of heart-healthy fats, including omega-3 fatty acids and monounsaturated fats.

Nutrient-rich: Nuts contain various vitamins and minerals, such as vitamin E, magnesium, and zinc, which contribute to overall well-being.

Satiety Support: The protein and healthy fats in nuts help keep you full and satisfied between meals, reducing the likelihood of overeating.

Creamy Hummus with Whole Wheat Pita

Prep Time: 10 minutes | No Cooking Required | Servings: 6

Ingredients

- 1 can (15 ounces) chickpeas, drained and rinsed

- 2 tablespoons tahini

- 2 tablespoons lemon juice

- 1 garlic clove, minced

- 1/2 teaspoon ground cumin

- Salt and pepper to taste

- 2 tablespoons olive oil

- Whole wheat pita bread, cut into wedges, for dipping

Instructions

1. In a food processor, blend the chickpeas, tahini, lemon juice, minced garlic, ground cumin, salt, and pepper until smooth.

2. While blending, drizzle in the olive oil until the hummus reaches the desired consistency.

3. Transfer the hummus to a bowl and serve with whole wheat pita wedges for a delightful dipping experience.

Health Benefits

Plant-Based Protein: Chickpeas, the main ingredient in hummus, are rich in plant-based protein that supports muscle health and provides sustained energy.

Fiber Content: Hummus is a good source of dietary fiber, which aids in digestion, stabilizes blood sugar levels, and supports heart health.

Vitamins and Minerals: Tahini, a component of hummus, offers calcium, iron, and B vitamins that contribute to bone health and overall vitality.

Cheese and Turkey Roll-Up Bites

Prep Time: 10 minute | No Cooking Required | Servings: 12

Ingredients

- 4 slices low-sodium turkey breast

- 4 slices reduced-fat Swiss cheese

- 1 small cucumber, cut into thin strips

- 1 red bell pepper, cut into thin strips

Instructions

1. Lay out the turkey slices on a clean surface.

2. Place a slice of Swiss cheese on each turkey slice.

3. Add cucumber and red bell pepper strips on top of the cheese.

4. Roll up the turkey slices with the fillings, securing them with toothpicks if needed.

5. Slice the roll-ups into bite-sized pieces and enjoy these protein-packed, crunchy bites.

Health Benefits

Protein Power: Turkey is a lean source of protein that supports muscle development and repair.

Calcium Source: Cheese provides calcium, essential for bone health, and protein that aids in satiety and energy balance.

Portable Snacking: Roll-up bites offer a convenient, portable, and satisfying snack option that helps prevent overindulgence.

With these Snacks in a Snap, you'll never have to resort to unhealthy snacking again. Whether you're craving something creamy, crunchy, or savory, these recipes have you covered. Keep your energy levels up and your taste buds satisfied with these quick and easy snack options that perfectly align with the South Beach Diet principles.

Overall Health Benefits Of Snacking

1. Steady Energy Levels: Well-balanced snacks can help maintain steady blood sugar levels throughout the day, preventing energy crashes and providing a sustained source of energy between meals.

2. **Appetite Control:** Having planned snacks can prevent overeating during main meals. Snacks with a good balance of protein, healthy fats, and fiber can keep you feeling full and satisfied, reducing the likelihood of excessive calorie consumption.

3. **Improved Nutrient Intake:** Snacking offers an opportunity to include additional servings of fruits, vegetables, whole grains, and lean proteins in your daily diet. This boosts your overall nutrient intake and supports optimal health.

4. **Enhanced Metabolism:** Consuming small, balanced snacks can keep your metabolism active, as the body continually works to digest and process food. This can contribute to better calorie burning throughout the day.

5. **Support for Weight Management:** Thoughtful snacking can prevent extreme hunger that often leads to unhealthy food choices. Opting for nutrient-dense snacks can help you manage your weight by curbing cravings and promoting better food decisions.

6. **Maintained Muscle Mass:** Protein-rich snacks can support muscle repair, maintenance, and growth. Adequate protein intake is essential for those engaged in physical activity or aiming to preserve muscle mass, especially as they age.

7. **Brain Function and Concentration:** Nutrient-dense snacks, particularly those rich in healthy fats, antioxidants, and omega-3 fatty acids, can support brain health. Omega-3s, for example, are known to enhance cognitive function and concentration.

8. Heart Health: Snacks that incorporate heart-healthy foods like nuts, seeds, whole grains, and fruits can help manage cholesterol levels, reduce inflammation, and support cardiovascular health.

9. Digestive Health: Snacks with fiber, such as fruits, vegetables, and whole grains, promote regular bowel movements and a healthy gut microbiome. Fiber aids in digestion and can alleviate digestive discomfort.

10. Reduced Risk of Overindulgence: Having planned snacks can prevent extreme hunger, which often leads to overeating or choosing less nutritious options. A well-timed snack can keep your appetite in check and prevent overindulgence later on.

11. Balanced Blood Sugar: Snacks with complex carbohydrates and protein can help stabilize blood sugar levels, reducing the risk of insulin spikes and dips.

12. Increased Micronutrient Intake: Nutrient-dense snacks, such as those rich in vitamins, minerals, and antioxidants, contribute to a well-rounded diet and may support immune function, skin health, and more.

13. Mood Regulation: Certain snacks, such as those containing dark chocolate or foods rich in tryptophan, can boost serotonin production and contribute to improved mood and relaxation.

Please Remember that the quality and quantity of snacks matter. Opt for whole, minimally processed foods that offer a balance of macronutrients and micronutrients. Additionally, portion control is key – try to aim for satisfying portions that prevent excessive calorie intake. By making mindful snack choices, you can reap these health benefits and enhance your overall well-being.

Chapter 3: LIGHT AND FRESH SALADS

Discover the art of salad-making with these Light and Fresh Salad recipes. These vibrant and nutrient-packed creations are not just ordinary salads; they're flavorful masterpieces that celebrate the colors, textures, and tastes of fresh ingredients. Say goodbye to bland and hello to a symphony of flavors that will leave you craving greens.

Grilled Chicken Caesar Salad

Prep Time: 15 minutes | Cook Time: 10 minutes | Serves: 2

Ingredients

- 2 boneless, skinless chicken breasts

- Salt and pepper to taste

- 1 tablespoon olive oil

- 1 large romaine lettuce heart, washed and chopped

- 1/4 cup grated Parmesan cheese

- Whole wheat croutons

- Caesar dressing (light or homemade)

Instructions

1. Season the chicken breasts with salt, pepper, and olive oil.

2. Grill the chicken on medium-high heat until cooked through, about 6-8 minutes per side. Let them rest before slicing.

3. In a large bowl, toss the chopped romaine lettuce with grated Parmesan cheese and whole wheat croutons.

4. Top the salad with sliced grilled chicken.

5. Drizzle with Caesar dressing and toss to combine. Serve immediately.

Health Benefits

Lean Protein: Grilled chicken provides a lean source of protein, which is essential for muscle repair, immune function, and maintaining a healthy weight.

Leafy Greens: The base of this salad often includes nutrient-rich greens like romaine lettuce, which offers vitamins A, C, and K, as well as fiber for digestion.

Healthy Fats: If included, a modest amount of Caesar dressing provides healthy fats from ingredients like olive oil and anchovies, contributing to heart health.

Tangy Mediterranean Cucumber Salad

Prep Time: 10 minutes | No Cooking Time Required | Serves: 4

Ingredients

- 2 large cucumbers, thinly sliced

- 1 cup cherry tomatoes, halved

- 1/2 red onion, thinly sliced

- 1/4 cup Kalamata olives, pitted and sliced

- 1/4 cup crumbled feta cheese

- 2 tablespoons extra-virgin olive oil

- 2 tablespoons red wine vinegar

- 1 teaspoon dried oregano

- Salt and pepper to taste

- Fresh parsley, chopped (for garnish)

Instructions

1. In a large bowl, combine the sliced cucumbers, cherry tomatoes, red onion, Kalamata olives, and crumbled feta cheese.

2. In a separate small bowl, whisk together the extra-virgin olive oil, red wine vinegar, dried oregano, salt, and pepper.

3. Drizzle the dressing over the salad and toss gently to coat all the ingredients.

4. Garnish with chopped fresh parsley and serve this tangy and refreshing Mediterranean delight.

Health Benefits

Hydration Support: Cucumbers have a high water content, helping to keep you hydrated and promote healthy skin.

Antioxidant-Rich: Ingredients like tomatoes, bell peppers, and olives are rich in antioxidants, which can help protect cells from damage and reduce inflammation.

Heart Health: Olives and olive oil are sources of monounsaturated fats, associated with improved cardiovascular health.

Colorful Cobb Salad with Avocado Dressing

Prep Time: 20 minutes | No Cooking Required | Serves: 2

Ingredients

- 4 cups mixed salad greens

- 1 cup cooked and diced chicken breast

- 1 hard-boiled egg, sliced

- 1/2 cup cherry tomatoes, halved

- 1/2 avocado, diced

- 1/4 cup crumbled blue cheese

- 2 slices turkey bacon, cooked and crumbled

Avocado Dressing

- 1 ripe avocado

- 1/4 cup plain Greek yogurt

- 2 tablespoons lime juice

- 2 tablespoons water

- Salt and pepper to taste

Instructions

1. Arrange the mixed salad greens on a large plate or bowl.

2. Assemble the diced chicken, hard-boiled egg slices, cherry tomatoes, diced avocado, crumbled blue cheese, and crumbled turkey bacon over the greens.

3. In a blender or food processor, blend the avocado, Greek yogurt, lime juice, water, salt, and pepper until smooth and creamy.

4. Drizzle the avocado dressing over the salad just before serving.

Health Benefits

Vitamin-Rich: Avocado, eggs, and various veggies in the salad provide an array of vitamins and minerals, including vitamin E, potassium, and B vitamins.

'Eggcellent' Protein: Hard-boiled eggs are a convenient source of protein and contain essential amino acids for various bodily functions.

Fiber and Satiety: The combination of protein, healthy fats from avocado, and fiber from vegetables promotes fullness and supports weight management.

Seared Tuna and Mixed Greens Delight

Prep Time: 15 minutes | Cook Time: 5 minutes | Serves: 2

Ingredients

- 2 tuna steaks

- Salt and pepper to taste

- 1 tablespoon sesame oil

- Mixed salad greens

- 1/2 cucumber, sliced

- 1/4 red onion, thinly sliced

- 1/4 cup edamame beans

- Sesame seeds (for garnish)

Soy-Ginger Dressing

- 3 tablespoons soy sauce (reduced-sodium)

- 1 tablespoon rice vinegar

- 1 teaspoon sesame oil

- 1 teaspoon honey

- 1 teaspoon grated fresh ginger

- 1 garlic clove, minced

Instructions

1. Season the tuna steaks with salt and pepper.

2. Heat sesame oil in a skillet over medium-high heat. Sear the tuna for about 1-2 minutes per side, or to your preferred level of doneness. Let it rest before slicing.

3. In a large bowl, combine mixed salad greens, cucumber slices, red onion slices, and edamame beans.

4. In a small bowl, whisk together the soy sauce, rice vinegar, sesame oil, honey, grated ginger, and minced garlic to make the dressing.

5. Drizzle the dressing over the salad and toss gently.

6. Top the salad with sliced seared tuna and garnish with sesame seeds.

Health Benefits

Omega-3 Fatty Acids: Tuna is a source of omega-3 fatty acids, which are beneficial for heart health, brain function, and reducing inflammation.

Iron and B Vitamins. Tuna provides essential nutrients like iron and B vitamins, supporting energy production and oxygen transport in the body.

Low-Calorie, High-Nutrient: Leafy greens and veggies offer a low-calorie way to pack in essential vitamins, minerals, and antioxidants.

Overall Health Benefits Of Incorporating Fresh Salads into Your Diet

1. Abundance of Nutrients: Fresh salads are typically loaded with a variety of vegetables, fruits, and other wholesome ingredients. These ingredients provide a wide range of essential vitamins, minerals, and antioxidants that support overall health.

2. Hydration: Many salad ingredients, such as cucumbers, lettuce, and watermelon, have high water content. Consuming water-rich foods helps keep you hydrated and supports various bodily functions.

3. **Fiber Boost:** Salads often contain fiber-rich foods like leafy greens, vegetables, fruits, and whole grains. Adequate fiber intake supports digestion, prevents constipation, and contributes to a healthy gut microbiome.

4. **Weight Management:** Eating a salad as a meal or part of a meal can promote feelings of fullness due to the fiber and water content. This can help control portion sizes and prevent overeating, aiding in weight management.

5. **Heart Health:** Many salad ingredients, such as leafy greens, tomatoes, and avocados, are heart-healthy foods. They are rich in antioxidants, healthy fats, and nutrients that support cardiovascular function and reduce the risk of heart disease.

6. **Blood Sugar Regulation:** Including low-glycemic index foods, such as leafy greens and non-starchy vegetables, in salads can help regulate blood sugar levels and prevent rapid spikes in glucose after meals.

7. **Improved Digestion:** Raw vegetables and fruits in salads contain enzymes that can aid digestion. Additionally, the fiber content supports regular bowel movements and a healthy digestive system.

8. **Skin Health:** The vitamins and antioxidants found in fresh salads, such as vitamins A and C, contribute to healthy skin. These nutrients promote collagen production, protect against oxidative stress, and maintain skin elasticity.

9. Reduced Inflammation: Ingredients commonly found in salads, such as leafy greens and berries, are rich in anti-inflammatory compounds. Consuming these foods can help reduce chronic inflammation in the body.

10. Bone Health: Dark leafy greens like kale and spinach are excellent sources of calcium and vitamin K, both of which are essential for maintaining strong and healthy bones.

11. Eye Health: Carotenoids like beta-carotene, found in orange and leafy green vegetables, are beneficial for eye health and may help reduce the risk of age-related macular degeneration.

12. Cancer Prevention: Antioxidants found in fruits and vegetables, such as vitamin C and flavonoids, have been linked to a reduced risk of certain types of cancers.

13. Improved Mood: The vitamins and minerals in salads, such as B vitamins, magnesium, and omega-3 fatty acids, support brain health and may contribute to improved mood and cognitive function.

14. Digestive Enzymes: Some raw vegetables contain enzymes that assist in breaking down food during digestion, potentially easing the digestive process.

15. Customizability: Salads are highly customizable, allowing you to tailor them to your taste preferences and dietary needs. This versatility makes it easy to include a wide variety of nutrient-rich foods.

Please remember that the nutritional content of your salad depends on the ingredients you choose. Make sure you go for a diverse range of colorful vegetables, lean proteins, healthy fats, and whole grains to maximize the health benefits that fresh salads can provide.

Chapter 4: QUICK & FLAVORFUL SEAFOOD

Dive into the depths of flavor with these Quick and Flavorful Seafood recipes. Packed with omega-3 fatty acids, lean protein, and an array of mouthwatering seasonings, these dishes are a testament to how seafood can be both nutritious and incredibly satisfying at the same time. From succulent shrimp to succulent salmon, get ready to embark on a culinary voyage through the seas.

Garlic-Lemon Shrimp Skewers

Prep Time: 15 minutes | Cook Time: 10 minutes | Servings: 4

Ingredients

- 1 pound large shrimp, peeled and deveined

- 2 tablespoons olive oil

- 2 cloves garlic, minced

- Zest and juice of 1 lemon

- 1 teaspoon dried oregano

- Salt and pepper to taste

- Wooden skewers, soaked in water

Instructions

1. In a bowl, combine the olive oil, minced garlic, lemon zest, lemon juice, dried oregano, salt, and pepper.

2. Thread the shrimp onto the soaked wooden skewers.

3. Brush the shrimp skewers with the garlic-lemon mixture, ensuring they are well coated.

4. Preheat a grill or grill pan over medium-high heat. Grill the shrimp skewers for about 2-3 minutes per side, until they are opaque and cooked through.

5. Serve these flavorful shrimp skewers hot, and consider pairing them with a side salad or whole grain for a complete meal.

Health Benefits

Lean Protein: Shrimp is a lean source of protein that supports muscle growth and repair.

Heart Health: Garlic contains allicin, a compound that may help lower blood pressure and reduce the risk of cardiovascular disease.

Immune Support: Lemon provides vitamin C, an antioxidant that strengthens the immune system and promotes skin health.

Pan-Seared Salmon with Dill Sauce

Prep Time: 10 minutes | Cook Time: 10 minutes| Servings: 4

Ingredients

- 2 salmon fillets

- Salt and pepper to taste

- 1 tablespoon olive oil

- 1 tablespoon fresh dill, chopped

- 2 tablespoons plain Greek yogurt

- 1 teaspoon Dijon mustard

- Juice of 1/2 lemon

Instructions

1. Season the salmon fillets with salt and pepper.

2. Heat the olive oil in a skillet over medium-high heat. Place the salmon fillets in the skillet, skin-side down.

3. Cook the salmon for about 3-4 minutes on each side, or until it flakes easily with a fork and is cooked to your desired level.

4. In a bowl, combine the chopped dill, Greek yogurt, Dijon mustard, and lemon juice to make the dill sauce.

5. Serve the pan-seared salmon hot, drizzled with the dill sauce.

Health Benefits

Omega-3 Fatty Acids: Salmon is rich in omega-3 fatty acids, which are beneficial for heart health, brain function, and reducing inflammation.

Bone Health: Vitamin D and calcium in salmon support bone health and may reduce the risk of osteoporosis.

Antioxidants: Dill contains antioxidants that have potential anti-inflammatory and anti-cancer properties.

Citrusy Mahi-Mahi Tacos

Prep Time: 20 minutes | Cook Time: 10 minutes | Servings: 4

Ingredients

- 2 mahi-mahi fillets

- Salt and pepper to taste

- 1 teaspoon ground cumin

- 1/2 teaspoon chili powder

- 2 tablespoons olive oil

- Juice of 1 lime

- Whole wheat tortillas

- Sliced avocado, for topping

- Fresh cilantro, chopped, for topping

- Red cabbage, shredded, for topping

Instructions

1. Season the mahi-mahi fillets with salt, pepper, ground cumin, and chili powder.

2. Heat the olive oil in a skillet over medium-high heat. Cook the mahi-mahi fillets
for about 3-4 minutes on each side, until they are cooked through and flake easily.

3. Squeeze lime juice over the cooked fillets.

4. Warm the whole wheat tortillas.

5. Assemble the tacos by placing pieces of cooked mahi-mahi in the tortillas. Top with sliced avocado, chopped cilantro, and shredded red cabbage.

6. Serve these zesty mahi-mahi tacos with an extra squeeze of lime juice.

Health Benefits

Vitamin-Rich: Mahi-mahi is a good source of vitamins B6 and B12, which support brain health, metabolism, and energy production.

Digestive Health: The fiber in whole wheat tortillas promotes healthy digestion and prevents constipation.

Bright Flavors: Citrus fruits like oranges in the salsa provide vitamin C and antioxidants for immune support.

Scallops in Brown Butter Sauce

Prep Time: 10 minutes | Cook Time: 10 minutes | Servings: 4

Ingredients

- 1 pound sea scallops

- Salt and pepper to taste

- 2 tablespoons unsalted butter

- 2 cloves garlic, minced

- Juice of 1/2 lemon

- Fresh parsley, chopped, for garnish

Instructions

1. Pat the scallops dry and season them with salt and pepper.

2. Heat a skillet over medium-high heat. Add the butter and let it melt and brown slightly.

3. Add the minced garlic to the skillet and sauté for about 1 minute, until fragrant.

4. Add the scallops to the skillet and cook for about 2-3 minutes on each side, until they are golden brown and opaque.

5. Squeeze lemon juice over the cooked scallops.

6. Garnish with chopped fresh parsley before serving these succulent scallops.

Health Benefits

Low-Calorie Protein: Scallops are rich in protein while being relatively low in calories, making them a weight-friendly protein source.

Healthy Fats: Brown butter sauce offers a rich flavor and small amounts of healthy fats, enhancing the taste of the dish.

B-Vitamins: Scallops contain B-vitamins, including B12 and folate, which contribute to nerve health, red blood cell formation, and energy metabolism.

Overall Health Benefits Of Incorporating Seafood Into Your Diet

1. **Rich in Omega-3 Fatty Acids:** Seafood, especially fatty fish like salmon, mackerel, and sardines, is a prime source of omega-3 fatty acids. These essential fats have been linked to heart health, reducing inflammation, and supporting brain function.

2. **Heart Health:** Omega-3 fatty acids found in seafood can help lower triglycerides, reduce blood pressure, and decrease the risk of heart disease by promoting healthy cholesterol levels and improving blood vessel function.

3. **Brain Health and Cognitive Function:** The omega-3 fatty acids EPA and DHA play a crucial role in brain health. Regular consumption of seafood has been associated with improved cognitive function, memory, and a reduced risk of cognitive decline.

4. **Eye Health:** Omega-3 fatty acids, particularly DHA, are important components of retinal cells. Regular consumption of seafood can help reduce the risk of age-related macular degeneration and support overall eye health.

5. **Protein Source:** Seafood is a lean source of high-quality protein, which is essential for muscle repair, growth, and overall body function.

6. **Vitamin and Mineral Content:** Seafood is rich in essential nutrients such as vitamin D, vitamin B12, iodine, selenium, and zinc. These nutrients contribute to bone health, immune function, thyroid health, and more.

7. **Low in Saturated Fat:** Most seafood is low in saturated fat, making it a heart-healthy choice that can help reduce the risk of cardiovascular disease.

8. **Anti-Inflammatory Properties:** Omega-3 fatty acids found in seafood have anti-inflammatory effects that may help alleviate chronic inflammation and reduce the risk of chronic diseases like arthritis and certain types of cancer.

9. **Improved Mood:** The omega-3s in seafood have been linked to improved mood and a reduced risk of depression. They can support the production of neurotransmitters that regulate mood.

10. **Aid in Weight Management:** Seafood is typically lower in calories than other protein sources like red meat. Including seafood in your diet can support weight loss and weight management efforts.

11. **Lower Risk of Autoimmune Diseases:** Regular consumption of omega-3-rich seafood has been associated with a reduced risk of autoimmune diseases like type 1 diabetes and rheumatoid arthritis.

12. **Reduced Risk of Stroke:** The omega-3 fatty acids in seafood can help reduce the risk of stroke by improving blood vessel function, decreasing blood clot formation, and lowering blood pressure.

13. Bone Health: Certain types of seafood, such as canned salmon with bones, are excellent sources of calcium and vitamin D, both of which are important for maintaining strong and healthy bones.

14. Pregnancy and Development: Omega-3 fatty acids are crucial for fetal brain and eye development during pregnancy. Consuming seafood, especially low-mercury options, supports a healthy pregnancy.

15. Anti-Aging: The nutrients and antioxidants found in seafood, such as vitamin E and selenium, contribute to healthy skin, hair, and overall anti-aging benefits.

Chapter 5: SPEEDY POULTRY DISHES

When time is of the essence, these quick and delightful poultry recipes will come to your rescue. Packed with lean protein and vibrant flavors, these dishes will satisfy your taste buds and keep you on track with your South Beach Diet goals.

Herb-Roasted Chicken with Asparagus

Prep Time: 10 minutes | Cook Time: 20 minutes | Serves: 4

Ingredients

- 4 boneless, skinless chicken breasts

- 1 bunch asparagus, trimmed

- 2 tablespoons olive oil

- 1 teaspoon dried thyme

- 1 teaspoon dried rosemary

- Salt and pepper to taste

Instructions

1. Preheat the oven to 400°F (200°C).

2. Place the chicken breasts on one side of a baking sheet and the trimmed asparagus on the other.

3. Drizzle olive oil over both the chicken and asparagus. Sprinkle with dried thyme, rosemary, salt, and pepper.

4. Toss the asparagus to coat it with the oil and spices, then spread it out evenly.

5. Roast in the preheated oven for about 20 minutes or until the chicken is cooked through and the asparagus is tender.

Turkey & Spinach Stuffed Portobello Mushrooms

Prep Time: 15 minutes | Cook Time: 15 minutes | Serves: 4

Ingredients

- 4 large Portobello mushrooms, stems removed

- 1 pound ground turkey

- 2 cups fresh spinach, chopped

- 1 small onion, finely chopped

- 2 cloves garlic, minced

- 1 teaspoon Italian seasoning

- Salt and pepper to taste

- ½ cup reduced-fat mozzarella cheese, shredded

Instructions

1. Preheat the oven to 375°F (190°C).

2. In a skillet over medium heat, cook the ground turkey until no longer pink. Add
the chopped onion and garlic, and cook until softened.

3. Stir in the chopped spinach and Italian seasoning. Cook until the spinach wilts.
Season with salt and pepper.

4. Place the Portobello mushrooms on a baking sheet. Divide the turkey and spinach mixture among the mushrooms, pressing it gently into the caps.

5. Sprinkle the shredded mozzarella cheese over the stuffed mushrooms.

6. Bake in the preheated oven for about 15 minutes or until the cheese is melted and bubbly.

Tangy Lemon-Turkey Stir-Fry

Prep Time: 15 minutes | Cook Time: 10 minutes | Serves: 4

Ingredients

- 1 pound turkey breast, thinly sliced

- 2 tablespoons low-sodium soy sauce

- 2 tablespoons lemon juice

- 1 tablespoon olive oil

- 1 red bell pepper, thinly sliced

- 1 yellow bell pepper, thinly sliced

- 1 cup snap peas, trimmed

- 2 cloves garlic, minced

- 1 teaspoon grated fresh ginger

- 2 green onions, chopped

- Sesame seeds for garnish (optional)

Instructions

1. In a bowl, mix together the soy sauce and lemon juice. Add the turkey slices and marinate for about 10 minutes.

2. Heat the olive oil in a large skillet or wok over high heat.

3. Add the marinated turkey slices and stir-fry for 2-3 minutes until cooked
through. Remove from the skillet and set aside.

4. In the same skillet, add the sliced bell peppers, snap peas, garlic, and ginger. Stir-fry for about 3-4 minutes until the vegetables are crisp-tender.

5. Return the cooked turkey to the skillet. Add chopped green onions and toss everything together.

6. Serve the stir-fry hot, garnished with sesame seeds if desired.

Rosemary Grilled Chicken Breasts

Prep Time: 10 minutes | Cook Time: 15 minutes | Serves: 4

Ingredients

- 4 boneless, skinless chicken breasts

2 tablespoons olive oil

- 2 tablespoons fresh rosemary, chopped

- 2 cloves garlic, minced

- Juice of 1 lemon

- Salt and pepper to taste

Instructions

1. Preheat the grill to medium-high heat.

2. In a bowl, combine olive oil, chopped rosemary, minced garlic, lemon juice, salt, and pepper.

3. Coat the chicken breasts with the rosemary mixture, ensuring they are well-covered.

4. Grill the chicken for about 6-7 minutes per side, or until the internal temperature reaches 165°F (74°C) and the chicken is no longer pink in the center.

5. Remove from the grill and let the chicken rest for a few minutes before serving.

Health Benefits Of Poultry Dishes

1. Lean Protein Source

Poultry, such as chicken and turkey, is an excellent source of lean protein. Protein is essential for building and repairing tissues, supporting muscle health, and boosting metabolism. Including lean poultry in your diet can help you maintain muscle mass, feel full and satisfied, and support healthy weight management.

2. Nutrient-Rich Ingredients

The dishes in this chapter incorporate various nutrient-rich ingredients like spinach, asparagus, bell peppers, and garlic. These ingredients are loaded with vitamins, minerals, and antioxidants that contribute to overall health. Spinach, for instance, is rich in iron and folate, while bell peppers provide a hefty dose of vitamin C.

3. Weight Management

Lean poultry dishes are often low in calories and high in protein, making them a great option for those looking to manage their weight. Protein-rich meals help control appetite and prevent overeating by promoting feelings of fullness and satisfaction.

4. Heart Health

The recipes emphasize using heart-healthy fats, such as olive oil, and incorporate lean protein sources. These factors can contribute to maintaining healthy cholesterol levels and reducing the risk of heart disease.

5. Blood Sugar Regulation

The recipes in this chapter are balanced in terms of macronutrients, which can help stabilize blood sugar levels. Lean proteins and fiber-rich vegetables like asparagus and bell peppers have a minimal impact on blood sugar, making these dishes suitable for those managing diabetes or looking to prevent blood sugar spikes.

6. Digestive Health

Many of the ingredients, including spinach, garlic, and ginger, are known for their potential digestive benefits. Garlic and ginger, for example, have been linked to improved digestion and reduced gastrointestinal discomfort.

7. Bone Health

Some recipes include herbs like rosemary, which not only add flavor but also provide potential bone health benefits. Rosemary contains compounds that may support bone density and strength.

8. Reduced Processed Ingredients

By preparing meals at home using fresh and wholesome ingredients, you have more control over the quality of the food you consume. This can help reduce your intake of processed foods, excessive sodium, and artificial additives.

9. Variety and Flavor

The recipes feature a variety of flavors, herbs, and spices, which can encourage a more diverse and enjoyable diet. This can help prevent palate fatigue and increase your overall satisfaction with your meals.

10. Time-Efficient Cooking
The recipes are designed to be prepared in under 30 minutes, making it easier for individuals with busy schedules to cook healthful meals at home. This encourages a habit of home cooking and reduces reliance on fast food or takeout.

Chapter 6: FAST AND SATISFYING MEATS

In this chapter, you'll discover an array of delicious meat-based dishes that are both quick to prepare and deeply satisfying. From succulent steak to tender pork and flavorful lamb, these recipes will ensure that your meals are not only convenient but also packed with protein and mouth watering flavors.

Peppered Sirloin Steak with Grilled Veggies

Prep Time: 10 minutes | Cook Time: 15 minutes | Serves: 4

Ingredients

- 4 sirloin steak cuts

- 2 tablespoons black peppercorns, crushed

- 2 tablespoons olive oil

- 1 red bell pepper, sliced

- 1 yellow bell pepper, sliced

- 1 zucchini, sliced

- Salt to taste

Instructions

1. Rub the crushed black peppercorns onto both sides of the sirloin steaks.

2. Heat the olive oil in a grill pan or skillet over medium-high heat.

3. Add the steaks and cook for about 4-5 minutes per side for medium-rare (adjust cooking time based on your preference).

4. While the steaks are cooking, grill the sliced bell peppers and zucchini until they're slightly charred and tender.

5. Season the grilled veggies with a pinch of salt.

6. Serve the peppered sirloin steaks alongside the grilled veggies for a satisfying and flavorful meal.

Health Benefits

Lean Protein Source: Sirloin steak is a lean cut of meat, rich in high-quality protein that supports muscle growth, repair, and overall body functions.

Iron Boost: Red meat like sirloin steak is an excellent source of heme iron, a type of iron that is more readily absorbed by the body. Adequate iron intake supports oxygen transport and energy production.

Vitamin-Packed Veggies: The grilled veggies accompanying the steak provide a range of essential vitamins and minerals, including fiber, vitamin C, and potassium. These nutrients promote digestion, immune health, and proper heart function.

Pork Tenderloin Medallions with Mustard Sauce

Prep Time: 10 minutes | Cook Time: 20 minutes | Serves: 4

Ingredients

- 1 pound pork tenderloin, cut into medallions

- 2 tablespoons olive oil

- 1 teaspoon dried thyme

- Salt and pepper to taste

Mustard Sauce

- 1/4 cup Dijon mustard

- 2 tablespoons honey

- 2 tablespoons apple cider vinegar

- 1 teaspoon minced fresh rosemary

Instructions

1. Season the pork medallions with dried thyme, salt, and pepper.

2. Heat olive oil in a skillet over medium-high heat.

3. Add the pork medallions and cook for about 4-5 minutes per side, until they're cooked through and nicely browned.

4. In a small bowl, whisk together the Dijon mustard, honey, apple cider vinegar, and minced rosemary to create the mustard sauce.

5. Serve the pork medallions drizzled with the mustard sauce.

Health Benefits

Lean and Flavorful: Pork tenderloin is a lean cut of pork that offers a tender and flavorful experience without excessive saturated fat. It provides high-quality protein and essential amino acids.

B Vitamins: Pork is a good source of B vitamins, including B6 and B12. These vitamins play a crucial role in energy metabolism, nerve function, and red blood cell formation.

Healthy Fats: The mustard sauce can be prepared using heart-healthy ingredients like olive oil. Including healthy fats in moderation supports brain health, skin integrity, and absorption of fat-soluble vitamins.

Lean Beef and Broccoli Stir-Fry

Prep Time: 15 minutes | Cook Time: 10 minutes | Serves: 4

Ingredients

- 1 pound lean beef, thinly sliced (such as sirloin or flank steak)

- 3 cups broccoli florets

- 2 tablespoons low-sodium soy sauce

- 1 tablespoon hoisin sauce

- 1 tablespoon oyster sauce

- 1 tablespoon sesame oil

- 2 cloves garlic, minced

- 1 teaspoon grated fresh ginger

- 1/4 teaspoon red pepper flakes (optional)

- 2 green onions, sliced

Instructions

1. In a bowl, combine the soy sauce, hoisin sauce, oyster sauce, sesame oil, and red pepper flakes if using. Set aside.

2. Heat a wok or large skillet over high heat.

3. Add a bit of oil to the pan, then add the minced garlic and grated ginger. Sauté for about 30 seconds.

4. Add the sliced beef and stir-fry for 2-3 minutes until it's no longer pink. Remove from the pan and set aside.

5. In the same pan, add a bit more oil if needed, and stir-fry the broccoli florets until they're vibrant green and tender-crisp.

6. Return the cooked beef to the pan. Pour the sauce over the beef and broccoli, and toss everything together until well-coated.

7. Garnish with sliced green onions before serving.

Health Benefits

Lean Protein Duo: Lean beef combined with broccoli creates a balanced meal with a complete protein profile, supplying all essential amino acids necessary for various bodily functions.

Omega-3 Fatty Acids: If grass-fed beef is used, you'll benefit from higher levels of omega-3 fatty acids, which are known for their anti-inflammatory properties and heart health benefits.

Cruciferous Powerhouse: Broccoli is a cruciferous vegetable rich in fiber, vitamins (C, K), and antioxidants. Its compounds have been associated with reduced cancer risk and improved digestion.

Flavor-Packed Lamb Chops

Prep Time: 10 minutes | Cook Time: 10 minutes | Serves: 4

Ingredients

- 8 lamb chops

- 2 tablespoons olive oil

- 2 cloves garlic, minced

- 1 teaspoon dried rosemary

- Salt and pepper to taste

Instructions

1. Preheat a grill or grill pan to medium-high heat.

2. In a bowl, mix together olive oil, minced garlic, dried rosemary, salt, and pepper.

3. Brush the lamb chops with the olive oil mixture, coating both sides.

4. Grill the lamb chops for about 3-4 minutes per side for medium-rare (adjust cooking time based on your preference).

5. Remove from the grill and let the lamb chops rest for a few minutes before serving.

Health Benefits

Rich Source of Protein: Lamb is a protein-rich meat that contains all essential amino acids, promoting muscle growth, tissue repair, and immune function.

Zinc Content: Lamb is notably rich in zinc, a mineral essential for immune health, wound healing, and proper sense of taste and smell.

Conjugated Linoleic Acid (CLA): Lamb from grass-fed sources may contain CLA, a type of healthy fat associated with reduced body fat, improved metabolic health, and anti-inflammatory effects.

Chapter 7: QUICK VEGGIE DIETS

In this chapter, we explore the world of vegetables turned into scrumptious and nutritious dishes that can be whipped up in no time. From vibrant stir-fries to innovative zucchini alternatives, these recipes are designed to make your mealtime both satisfying and healthful, in alignment with the principles of the South Beach Diet.

Garlic-Ginger Stir-Fried Vegetables

Prep Time: 10 minutes | Cook Time: 10 minutes | Serves:

Ingredients

- 2 cups mixed vegetables (broccoli florets, bell peppers, snap peas, carrots), sliced

- 2 tablespoons low-sodium soy sauce

- 1 tablespoon sesame oil

- 1 teaspoon fresh ginger, grated

- 2 cloves garlic, minced
- 1 teaspoon honey or sweetener of choice

- 1 tablespoon olive oil

- 1 teaspoon sesame seeds (optional)

- Salt and pepper to taste

Instructions

1. In a small bowl, whisk together the soy sauce, sesame oil, grated ginger, minced garlic, and honey.

2. Heat olive oil in a large skillet or wok over high heat.

3. Add the sliced vegetables to the skillet and stir-fry for about 4-5 minutes until they are slightly tender but still crisp.

4. Pour the prepared sauce over the vegetables and toss to coat evenly. Continue to stir-fry for another 2-3 minutes.

5. Season with salt and pepper, and sprinkle with sesame seeds if desired.

6. Serve the stir-fried vegetables as a side dish or over brown rice or quinoa.

Mediterranean Zucchini Noodle

Prep Time: 15 minutes | Cook Time: 5 minutes | Serves: 2

Ingredients

- 2 medium zucchinis, spiralized into noodles

- 1 tablespoon olive oil

- 1 cup cherry tomatoes, halved

- ½ cup Kalamata olives, pitted and sliced

- ¼ cup crumbled feta cheese

- 2 tablespoons fresh basil, chopped

- 1 tablespoon lemon juice

- Salt and pepper to taste

Instructions

1. Heat olive oil in a skillet over medium heat.

2. Add the zucchini noodles and sauté for about 3-4 minutes until they are just
tender. Avoid overcooking to maintain a slight crunch.

3. Remove the skillet from heat and transfer the zucchini noodles to a serving dish.

4. Toss the zucchini noodles with halved cherry tomatoes, sliced Kalamata olives, crumbled feta cheese, and chopped fresh basil.

5. Drizzle with lemon juice and season with salt and pepper.

6. Serve the Mediterranean zucchini noodles as a light and refreshing main dish
or as a side alongside grilled protein.

Spicy Roasted Cauliflower Bites

Prep Time: 10 minutes | Cook Time: 20 minutes | Serves: 4

Ingredients

- 1 head cauliflower, cut into florets

- 2 tablespoons olive oil

- 1 teaspoon paprika

- ½ teaspoon cayenne pepper (adjust to taste)

- 1 teaspoon garlic powder

- Salt and pepper to taste

- Fresh parsley, chopped, for garnish

Instructions

1. Preheat the oven to 425°F (220°C) and line a baking sheet with parchment paper.

2. In a large bowl, toss the cauliflower florets with olive oil, paprika, cayenne pepper, garlic powder, salt, and pepper until evenly coated.

3. Spread the seasoned cauliflower in a single layer on the prepared baking sheet.

4. Roast in the preheated oven for about 20 minutes, tossing halfway through, until the cauliflower is golden and tender.

5. Remove from the oven and sprinkle with chopped fresh parsley before serving.

6. Enjoy the spicy roasted cauliflower bites as a flavorful side dish or as a satisfying snack.

Creamy Spinach and Artichoke Casserole

Prep Time: 15 minutes | Cook Time: 20 minutes | Serves: 4

Ingredients

- 1 tablespoon olive oil

- 1 small onion, chopped

- 2 cloves garlic, minced

- 10 ounces frozen chopped spinach, thawed and drained

- 1 (14-ounce) can artichoke hearts, drained and chopped

- ½ cup low-fat Greek yogurt

- ½ cup reduced-fat cream cheese

- ¼ cup grated Parmesan cheese

- ½ teaspoon red pepper flakes (adjust to taste)

- Salt and pepper to taste

- ¼ cup grated mozzarella cheese (optional, for topping)

Instructions

1. Preheat the oven to 375°F (190°C).

2. Heat olive oil in a skillet over medium heat. Add chopped onion and garlic, and sauté until softened.

3. Stir in the chopped spinach and artichoke hearts, and cook for a few minutes until heated through.

4. In a bowl, mix the Greek yogurt, cream cheese, grated Parmesan cheese, red pepper flakes, salt, and pepper.

5. Combine the yogurt and cheese mixture with the spinach and artichoke mixture in the skillet. Mix well.

6. Transfer the mixture to a baking dish. If desired, sprinkle grated mozzarella cheese on top.

7. Bake in the preheated oven for about 20 minutes or until the casserole is bubbly and slightly golden on top.

8. Serve the creamy spinach and artichoke casserole as a flavorful and satisfying side dish.

Overall Health Benefits

1. Nutrient-Rich Wellness

2. Fiber for Digestive Health

3. Disease-Fighting Phytonutrients

4. Weight Management and Satiety

5. Heart Health and Blood Pressure

6. Antioxidant Defense

7. Blood Sugar Regulation

8. Bone Health and Vitality

9. Hydration and Skin Radiance

10. Culinary Tips for Retaining Nutrients

These quick veggie delights showcase the versatility of vegetables and how they can shine as both supporting characters and stars of your meals. With these recipes, you'll have a variety of ways to incorporate more vegetables into your diet while enjoying the convenience of quick and easy preparation.

Chapter 8: SPEEDY SIDES

In this chapter, you'll discover a variety of quick and delicious side dishes that perfectly complement your main courses. These sides are not only nutritious but also bursting with flavor, adding an extra touch of satisfaction to your meals.

Quinoa Pilaf with Mixed Herbs

Prep Time: 10 minutes | Cooking Time: 15 minutes | Servings: 4

Ingredients

- 1 cup quinoa, rinsed and drained

- 2 cups low-sodium chicken or vegetable broth

- 1 tablespoon olive oil

- 2 cloves garlic, minced

- 1/4 cup mixed fresh herbs (such as parsley, thyme, and chives), chopped

- Salt and pepper to taste

Instructions

1. In a medium saucepan, heat the olive oil over medium heat. Add the minced garlic and sauté for about 1 minute until fragrant.

2. Add the quinoa to the saucepan and toast it for another 2 minutes, stirring occasionally.

3. Pour in the chicken or vegetable broth and bring to a boil. Reduce the heat to low, cover, and let it simmer for 15-20 minutes, or until the quinoa is cooked and the liquid is absorbed.

4. Once cooked, fluff the quinoa with a fork and stir in the mixed herbs. Season with salt and pepper to taste.

5. Serve the quinoa pilaf as a nutritious and flavorful side dish.

Health Benefits

High-Quality Protein: Quinoa is a complete protein source, containing all nine essential amino acids, making it suitable for vegetarians and vegans.

Fiber-Rich: It is also rich in dietary fiber, aiding digestion, promoting a feeling of fullness, and supporting gut health.

Nutrient-Dense: As a dish, Quinoa provides essential nutrients like magnesium, iron, and B vitamins for energy production and overall health.

Steamed Asparagus with Lemon Zest

Prep Time: 5 minutes | Cooking Time: 8 minutes | Servings: 4

Ingredients

- 1 bunch of asparagus, tough ends trimmed

- Zest of 1 lemon

- 1 tablespoon olive oil

- Salt and pepper to taste

Instructions

1. Prepare a steamer basket over a pot of boiling water.

2. Place the trimmed asparagus in the steamer basket and cover. Steam for about
3-4 minutes until the asparagus is tender but still crisp.

3. Remove the asparagus from the steamer and transfer to a serving platter.

4. Drizzle olive oil over the steamed asparagus and sprinkle with lemon zest.

5. Season with salt and pepper to taste. Toss gently to coat.

6. Serve the steamed asparagus with lemon zest as a vibrant and refreshing side dish.

Health Benefits

Antioxidant-Rich: Asparagus is loaded with antioxidants like vitamin C, vitamin E, and glutathione, which help protect cells from oxidative stress and inflammation.

Digestive Support: Asparagus contains dietary fiber and prebiotics that promote healthy digestion and support the growth of beneficial gut bacteria.

B Vitamins: Asparagus is a good source of B vitamins, including folate, which is important for cell division and a healthy cardiovascular system.

Cheesy Broccoli Bake

Indulge in a guilt-free cheesy delight with this broccoli bake. Steamed broccoli florets are smothered in a creamy, low-fat cheese sauce and baked to perfection. A sprinkle of whole wheat breadcrumbs on top adds a satisfying crunch.

Prep Time: 10 minutes | Cooking Time: 20 minutes | Servings: 6

Ingredients

- 4 cups broccoli florets

- 1/2 cup low-fat cottage cheese

- 1/4 cup grated Parmesan cheese

- 1/4 teaspoon garlic powder

- Salt and pepper to taste

- Cooking spray

Instructions

1. Preheat the oven to 375°F (190°C). Grease a baking dish with cooking spray.

2. Steam the broccoli florets for about 3-4 minutes until they are bright green and slightly tender. Drain any excess water.

3. In a blender or food processor, combine the cottage cheese, grated Parmesan cheese, garlic powder, salt, and pepper. Blend until smooth and creamy.

4. Place the steamed broccoli in the greased baking dish. Pour the cheese mixture over the broccoli, coating it evenly.

5. Bake in the preheated oven for 15-20 minutes, or until the top is golden and bubbly.

6. Remove from the oven and let it cool slightly before serving.

7. Serve the cheesy broccoli bake as a comforting and nutritious side dish.

Health Benefits

Calcium and Vitamin K: Broccoli is rich in calcium and vitamin K, contributing to bone health and proper blood clotting.

Detoxification Support: Compounds in broccoli, such as sulforaphane, support the body's detoxification processes and may have potential anti-cancer properties.

Immune Boost: Broccoli provides vitamin C and other antioxidants that support the immune system's function.

Cumin-Spiced Sweet Potato Wedges

Transform sweet potatoes into delectable wedges that are seasoned with a blend of cumin, paprika, and a touch of cayenne for a hint of heat. These crispy wedges are a wholesome alternative to regular fries.

Prep Time: 10 minutes | Cooking Time: 25 minutes | Servings: 4

Ingredients

- 4 cups broccoli florets

- 1/2 cup low-fat cottage cheese

- 1/4 cup grated Parmesan cheese

- 1/4 teaspoon garlic powder

- Salt and pepper to taste

- Cooking spray

Instructions

1. Preheat the oven to 375°F (190°C). Grease a baking dish with cooking spray.

2. Steam the broccoli florets for about 3-4 minutes until they are bright green and slightly tender. Drain any excess water.

3. In a blender or food processor, combine the cottage cheese, grated Parmesan cheese, garlic powder, salt, and pepper. Blend until smooth and creamy.

4. Place the steamed broccoli in the greased baking dish. Pour the cheese mixture over the broccoli, coating it evenly.

5. Bake in the preheated oven for about 15-20 minutes, or until the top is golden and bubbly.

6. Remove from the oven and let it cool slightly before serving.

7. Serve the cheesy broccoli bake as a comforting and nutritious side dish.

Health Benefits

Beta-carotene: Sweet potatoes are high in beta-carotene, a precursor to vitamin A, which supports vision, skin health, and immune function.

Complex Carbohydrates: Sweet potatoes offer complex carbohydrates for sustained energy release and blood sugar control.

Anti-Inflammatory: The spice cumin has anti-inflammatory properties that may contribute to reduced inflammation and improved digestive health.

Each side dish in this chapter is designed to be simple to prepare, allowing you to focus on enjoying your meal while still reaping the nutritional benefits of wholesome ingredients. Whether you're serving up a weeknight dinner or entertaining guests, these speedy sides will impress with their taste and ease of preparation.

Chapter 9: EFFORTLESS DESERTS

When it comes to desserts, you don't need to spend hours in the kitchen to satisfy your sweet tooth while staying true to the principles of the South Beach Diet. These quick and easy dessert recipes are designed to bring a touch of indulgence to your meals without compromising your health goals. From fruity parfaits to creamy mousses, these desserts will have you enjoying guilt-free treats in no time.

Mixed Berry Parfait with Whipped Cream

Prep Time: 15 minutes | No Cooking Required | Servings: 4

Ingredients

- 1 cup mixed berries (strawberries, blueberries, raspberries)

- 1 cup low-fat Greek yogurt

- 2 tablespoons chopped nuts (almonds, walnuts)

- 1 teaspoon honey (optional)

- 1/2 teaspoon vanilla extract

- Lightly whipped cream for topping

Instructions

1. Mix the Greek yogurt with vanilla extract and honey (if used) until well combined.

2. In serving glasses, layer the yogurt mixture, mixed berries, and chopped nuts.

3. Repeat the layers until the glasses are filled, finishing with a layer of berries and a dollop of lightly whipped cream on top.

4. Serve immediately or refrigerate until ready to enjoy.

Dark Chocolate Avocado Mousse

Prep Time: 10 minutes | No Cooking Required| Servings: 2

Ingredients

- 2 ripe avocados, peeled and pitted

- 1/4 cup unsweetened cocoa powder

- 1/4 cup sugar-free sweetener (such as erythritol or stevia)

- 1 teaspoon vanilla extract

- Pinch of salt

- Dark chocolate shavings for garnish (optional)

Instructions

1. In a food processor, blend the avocados, cocoa powder, sugar-free sweetener, vanilla extract, and salt until smooth and creamy.

2. Taste and adjust sweetness if needed by adding more sweetener.

3. Spoon the mousse into serving bowls or glasses.

4. If desired, garnish with dark chocolate shavings.

5. Chill in the refrigerator for at least 15 minutes before serving.

Baked Apples with Cinnamon and Walnuts

Prep Time: 10 minutes | Cooking Time: 20 minutes | Servings: 4

Ingredients

- 2 apples, cored and halved

- 2 tablespoons chopped walnuts

- 1 teaspoon ground cinnamon

- 1 teaspoon coconut oil

- 1 teaspoon sugar-free sweetener

- Dash of nutmeg

Instructions

1. Preheat the oven to 350°F (175°C).

2. Place the apple halves in a baking dish, cut side up.

3. Mix the chopped walnuts, ground cinnamon, coconut oil, sugar-free sweetener, and nutmeg in a small bowl.

4. Fill the apple halves with the walnut mixture.

5. Bake in the preheated oven for 15-20 minutes or until the apples are tender.

6. Remove from the oven and let cool slightly before serving.

Chia Seed Pudding with Vanilla

Prep Time: 5 minutes (plus chilling time) | No Cooking Required|
Servings: 2

Ingredients

- 1/4 cup chia seeds

- 1 cup unsweetened almond milk

- 1/2 teaspoon vanilla extract

- 1 teaspoon sugar-free sweetener

- Fresh berries for topping

Instructions

1. In a bowl, whisk together the chia seeds, almond milk, vanilla extract, and sugar-free sweetener.

2. Let the mixture sit for about 5 minutes, then whisk again to prevent clumping.

3. Cover the bowl and refrigerate for at least 15-20 minutes or until the mixture thickens and forms a pudding-like consistency.

4. Before serving, give the pudding a good stir and divide it into serving cups.

5. Top with fresh berries and enjoy!

Health Benefits

1. Controlled Sugar Intake: The desserts in this chapter are likely to use natural sweeteners like fruits, berries, and a controlled amount of honey or maple syrup. This approach helps in managing blood sugar levels more effectively compared to desserts with refined sugars.

2. Rich in Antioxidants: Many of the desserts may incorporate berries, dark chocolate, and nuts, which are rich in antioxidants. Antioxidants help combat oxidative stress and inflammation in the body, potentially reducing the risk of chronic diseases.

3. Heart Health: Dark chocolate, avocados (used in chocolate avocado mousse), and nuts are ingredients that can positively impact heart health. These ingredients are known to support healthy cholesterol levels and improve cardiovascular function.

4. Fiber Intake: Desserts with ingredients like chia seeds, berries, and apples can contribute to dietary fiber intake. Fiber aids digestion, helps maintain a feeling of fullness, and supports gut health.

5. Healthy Fats: Avocado and nuts are sources of healthy fats, including monounsaturated and polyunsaturated fats. These fats are beneficial for overall health, including brain function, skin health, and hormone regulation.

6. Nutrient Density: The desserts may incorporate nutrient-dense ingredients like nuts, seeds, and fruits. Nutrient-dense foods provide essential vitamins, minerals, and micronutrients that contribute to overall well-being.

7. Weight Management: Healthier dessert options can fit into a balanced diet and support weight management goals. By satisfying sweet cravings with these desserts, individuals are less likely to overindulge in high-calorie, low-nutrient options.

8. Digestive Health: Chia seed pudding and fruits used in desserts can promote digestive health due to their soluble fiber content. They can help prevent constipation and support a healthy gut microbiome.

9. Mindful Eating: Including satisfying and flavorful desserts that are also nutritious encourages mindful eating. People can enjoy their treats while being aware of portion sizes and flavors, fostering a healthier relationship with food.

10. Reduced Guilt: Healthier dessert options can provide the enjoyment of sweets without the associated guilt. This can contribute to a more positive attitude toward food and eating.

It's very important to note that these desserts are not only delicious but also designed to fit within the South Beach Diet principles. Feel free to adjust the ingredients and portions based on your dietary preferences and needs. Enjoy these quick and easy desserts guilt-free!

Chapter 10: REFRESHING BEVERAGES

In the midst of our fast-paced lives, staying hydrated and energized is essential. These refreshing beverage recipes offer delightful sips that not only quench your thirst but also provide a boost of flavor and nutrition. From revitalizing teas to invigorating infused waters and protein-packed shakes, this chapter will keep you cool, satisfied, and on track with your health goals.

Minty Green Tea Cooler

Prep Time: 5 minutes | Cooking Time: 5 minutes (for steeping) | Servings: 2

Ingredients

- 2 green tea bags

- 1 cup fresh mint leaves

- 1 lemon, sliced

- 4 cups cold water

- Ice cubes

Instructions

1. Brew the green tea bags in 2 cups of boiling water. Allow it to steep for 5 minutes, then remove the tea bags and let the tea cool.

2. In a pitcher, combine the brewed green tea, mint leaves, and lemon slices.

3. Add cold water and stir well. Refrigerate for at least an hour to let the flavors infuse.

4. Serve over ice and garnish with extra mint leaves and lemon slices

Health Benefits

- *Green tea* is rich in antioxidants called catechins, which have been linked to various health benefits, including improved heart health and reduced inflammation.

- Adding mint can aid digestion and provide a refreshing, soothing sensation.

Sparkling Berry Infusion

Prep Time: 10 Minutes | No Cooking Required | Servings: 4

Ingredients

- 1 cup mixed berries (strawberries, blueberries, raspberries)

- 1 tablespoon honey (optional)

- 1 lemon, juiced

- Sparkling water

- Fresh basil leaves, for garnish

Instructions

1. In a bowl, gently mash the mixed berries with a fork. If desired, stir in honey for added sweetness.

2. Divide the mashed berries into glasses, squeezing in the lemon juice evenly.

3. Fill each glass with sparkling water, stirring gently to combine.

4. Garnish with fresh basil leaves and extra berries.

Health Benefits

- *Berries* are packed with vitamins, minerals, and antioxidants that support immune health and may reduce the risk of chronic diseases.

- *Sparkling water* provides hydration without added sugars, making it a healthier alternative to sugary sodas.

Citrus-Basil Spa Water

Prep Time: 5 minutes | No Cooking Required | Servings: 6

Ingredients

- 1 orange, sliced

- 1 lime, sliced

- 1 lemon, sliced

- Handful of fresh basil leaves

- Ice cubes

- Water

Instructions

1. In a large pitcher, combine the orange, lime, and lemon slices.

2. Tear the fresh basil leaves and add them to the pitcher.

3. Fill the pitcher with water and add ice cubes.

4. Allow the water to sit for about 10 minutes before serving to allow the flavors to infuse.

Health Benefits

- *Citrus fruits* like lemon, lime, and orange are excellent sources of vitamin C, which supports skin health, immune function, and collagen production.

- *Basil* is rich in essential oils with potential anti-inflammatory and antimicrobial properties.

Iced Coffee Protein Shake

Prep Time: 5 minutes | No Cooking Required | Servings: 1

Ingredients

- 1 cup chilled brewed coffee

- 1 scoop vanilla protein powder

- 1 tablespoon almond butter

- 1 teaspoon unsweetened cocoa powder

- ½ banana, frozen

- Ice cubes

Instructions

1. In a blender, combine the chilled coffee, vanilla protein powder, almond butter,
cocoa powder, frozen banana, and a handful of ice cubes.

2. Blend on high until smooth and creamy.

3. Pour into a glass and enjoy as a satisfying and energizing pick-me-up.

Health Benefits

- *Coffee* is a source of caffeine, which can enhance alertness and cognitive function when consumed in moderation.

- *Protein shakes* can aid in muscle recovery and maintenance, making this a great option after workouts

Appendix

Food List for the South Beach Diet Phases:

In this section, you'll find a comprehensive food list that aligns with the different phases of the South Beach Diet. Whether you're in Phase 1, Phase 2, or Phase 3, this list will help you choose the right foods to meet your nutritional goals. From lean proteins to healthy fats and fiber-rich carbohydrates, the food list provides options for balanced and delicious meals.

Phase 1:

During Phase 1 of the South Beach Diet, focus on eliminating sugars and starches to stabilize blood sugar levels and kickstart weight loss. Enjoy a variety of lean proteins, non-starchy vegetables, and healthy fats.

Allowed Foods:

- *Lean proteins:* Chicken, turkey, lean beef, pork, fish, shellfish

- *Vegetables:* Leafy greens, broccoli, cauliflower, asparagus, spinach, bell peppers, cucumbers, zucchini

- *Healthy fats:* Olive oil, avocado, nuts (in moderation)

- *Dairy:* Low-fat or fat-free Greek yogurt, low-fat cheese

- *Legumes:* Black beans, kidney beans, chickpeas (in moderation)

- *Nuts and seeds (in moderation):* Almonds, walnuts, flaxseeds

Phase 2:

Phase 2 gradually reintroduces certain whole grains and fruits while continuing to focus on lean proteins and vegetables. This phase aims to achieve steady weight loss.

Allowed Foods (in addition to Phase 1 foods):

- *Whole grains:* Quinoa, whole wheat pasta, brown rice, barley

- *Fruits:* Berries, apples, pears, oranges, melons (in moderation)

- *Additional vegetables:* Carrots, sweet potatoes, peas, corn (in moderation)

- *Limited alcohol:* Dry wine, light beer (in moderation)

Phase 3:

Phase 3 is the maintenance phase where you've reached your weight loss goals and are focused on sustaining a healthy lifestyle. You can continue enjoying foods from Phase 1 and Phase 2, with added flexibility.

Allowed Foods (in addition to Phase 1 & Phase 2 foods):

- *Other whole grains:* Oats, whole grain bread (in moderation)

- *More fruits:* All fruits in moderation

- *Occasional treats:* Dark chocolate (70% cocoa or higher), dessert on special occasions

General Guidelines:

- Drink plenty of water throughout all phases.

- Use herbs, spices, and healthy condiments to add flavor to your dishes.

- Avoid processed foods, sugary snacks, and foods high in saturated fats.

- Monitor portion sizes to maintain balanced meals.

Note: Individual dietary needs and health conditions may vary. Please Consult with a healthcare professional before making significant changes to your diet.

Cooking Tips and Techniques:

Cooking is both an art and a science, and mastering certain techniques can elevate your culinary creations to new heights. Whether you're a seasoned chef or just starting out, these cooking tips will help you achieve delicious results every time you step into the kitchen.

1. Seasoning for Flavor:

   - Season your dishes at different stages of cooking for layered flavors. Add salt and pepper early on and adjust seasoning as needed.

   - Experiment with herbs, spices, and citrus zest to add depth and complexity to your meals.

2. Perfecting the Sear:

   - To achieve a perfect sear on meats, make sure the pan is hot before adding the meat. This ensures a nice caramelized crust.

   - Avoid overcrowding the pan, as this can lead to steaming instead of searing. Cook in batches if necessary.

3. Balancing Sweet and Savory:

   - Enhance the flavors of savory dishes with a touch of sweetness. Add a drizzle of honey or a sprinkle of dried fruits to complement salty or umami flavors.

4. Mastering Steaming:

   - Steaming vegetables preserves their nutrients and vibrant colors. Use a steamer basket or microwave-safe dish with a bit of water to steam veggies quickly.

5. Monitoring Doneness:

   - Invest in a meat thermometer to ensure your proteins are cooked to the right internal temperature, avoiding undercooked or overcooked results.

6. Playing with Textures:

   - Combine different textures in a dish for an enjoyable eating experience. Pair crispy components with creamy ones to create contrast.

7. Building Layers in One-Pot Meals:

   - When making one-pot dishes, start by sautéing aromatics like onions and garlic. Add proteins, then liquids, and finally grains or vegetables for layered flavors.

8. Utilizing Citrus:

   - Citrus juices and zests can brighten up dishes. Add a squeeze of lemon or lime to finish a dish and balance flavors.

9. Resting and Carrying Over:

- Allow meats to rest after cooking before slicing. This lets juices redistribute for a juicier result. Note that meats continue cooking slightly after being removed from the heat.

10. Mindful Ingredient Prep:

- Prepare all your ingredients before starting to cook ("mise en place"). This saves time and ensures a smoother cooking process.

Cooking is about creativity and learning. Don't be afraid to experiment, adapt, and personalize recipes to suit your preferences. With practice, you'll gain confidence and refine your skills to become a more proficient and creative cook.

Measurement Conversions:

Converting measurements can sometimes be a hassle, especially when dealing with different units. This section provides a handy conversion guide for common cooking measurements, ensuring that you can easily switch between metric and imperial units. From teaspoons to cups and grams to ounces, these conversions will simplify your cooking process.

Volume Conversions:

Measurement	Imperial	Metric
1 teaspoon	1 tsp	5 ml
1 tablespoon	1 tbsp	15 ml
1 fluid ounce	1 fl oz	30 ml
1 cup	1 cup	240 ml
1 pint	1 pt	473 ml
1 quart	1 qt	946 ml
1 gallon	1 gal	3.785 L

Weight Conversions:

Measurement	Imperial	Metric
1 ounce	1 oz	28.35 g
1 pound	1 lb	453.59 g
1 gram	-	0.035 oz
100 grams	-	3.53 oz
1 kilogram	-	2.205 lbs

Temperature Conversions:

Measurement	Fahrenheit	Celsius
Freezing point	32°F	0°C
Boiling point	212°F	100°C
Room temperature	68-72°F	20-22°C
Oven moderate	350°F	175°C
Oven hot	400°F	200°C
Oven very hot	450°F	230°C

Length Conversions:

Measurement	Imperial	Metric
1 inch	1 in	2.54 cm
1 foot	1 ft	30.48 cm
1 yard	1 yd	0.914 m
1 mile	1 mi	1.609 km

Printed in Great Britain
by Amazon

37600974R00084